Fragments of my Imagination

Skeeter Smith

Fragments of my Imagination

Table of Contents

What Others Are Saying:

"Skeeter's poetry can be very deep and thought provoking. At times, gives me just what I need, a good laugh." – T. Taylor

"I am not much into poetry, but what Skeeter writes is all about life challenges and choices. Her stories share bittersweet and sweet experiences throughout. As well as serious, she can be quite funny with her storytelling." – M. Smith

"Different roads do not mean you are lost. Just means you have a different story to tell. Skeeter's poetry shows that not just one path is the only path." – T. Peters

"Skeeter has a poignant paradigm that allows her to see past superficial ideas and digs deep into the heart of the matter of her writing." – D. Villa

"Skeeter isn't afraid to share fragile experiences. Open and transparent, she writes from the only place she knows, her very soul." – M. Kirksey

SHINE ON WOMAN

I looked upon you and saw magic. My eyes devoured your goodness and knew you as Mother. The kindest of kind; a divine creator or worlds.

~ABIDE~

Meteors collide and stars abide

Because you are infinite,

Endless,

Possibilities.

Because you exist,

Precious and divine.

~AGAIN AND AGAIN~

A sudden stillness

Beats my heart.

You left me standing

Waving in the dark.

To enter a home

All alone,

Because you were here,

And now you are gone.

Pounding exposition,

Realizing this fear,

Has gripped me blindly

Because you are not here.

Seems too empty

Once was not so,

But you came and went,

And now I know.

Hours we spend talking

Sharing our words.

A love language of time,

Together...

No thought to discourage.

And if that day comes again,

You join me to make amends,

May we find each other...

Again,

And again.

Just for today... May your day begin
with profound gratitude for everything
that is good in your life. May your
day end with prayers of gratitude for
what has blessed you today.

~HERE~

When you are not here,

And you are there.

When you are not here or there

You cannot be everywhere.

Why try to be

All those places

In those spaces...

You are not meant to be?

To be here,

You cannot be there

Still, anywhere is better than nowhere.

~WONDER~

I know you struggle

To make amends.

A daily fortress

Of starting again.

Still, you persist

Make it work

A kind word

A gentle touch.

I look in wonder

At your reserve.

Inspiring to watch

Even on your last nerve.

Patient and resilient

It all gets done.

As you muddle

Through your daily

Awesomeness sprung.

Sleep deprived and struggling

You get it done.

I look on in wonder

At the mother and woman

You have become.

~WRAP AROUND PORCH~

When I dream of all I desire

My dream begins with a home

Nestled in some trees

A wrap around porch

For you and for me.

Wisteria blessing

Purple blooms galore

Jasmine in the air

Cat purring on my lap

Dog by my rocking chair.

We sit in silence

Gazing at each star.

Wind rustles through the trees.

Cicadas beckon in one accord

The moon sits not far.

Sacred moments

You and me alone

Near our fondest allies

At home.

And my wrap around porch

A view all around

The sound of nighttime

Nothing more to expound.

Here in silence

I give thanks for the day

The sweet smell of honeysuckle

Drifting in the night breeze.

Oh, the gladness

To know I reside

Only this moment

My wrap around porch to abide.

~REMIND ME~

Remind me,

If I forget

To love myself

Be more gentle,

Life is not a test.

Strengthen my 'wallows'

Tender with my sorrows,

Filter unloving thoughts,

Cultivate only fertile

Feelings to inspire.

Remind me,

If I forget

Love for me

Never regrets.

Remind me,

If I forget,

Created in His image

To reflect.

Infinite love

No delay,

Capacity to engender

Love for me,

Love infinitely.

Gratitude lights the day -
Gratitude lights the way.

~WOMAN OF FIRE~

She is fire

Burns bright

Turns nighttime

Into daylight.

Touch her

Reach out

She will turn

Your molten hand

Into desire.

Honor her flame

She burns Kelvin

Too hot to ignite.

Black ashes will never be her dust.

Her fire lifts the sky.

Scorches,

Lights galaxies

Eclipses eternity.

~GROWTH~

The hardest inside job

Personal improvement to the extreme

The first step is to become aware

Limitations and blind spots

Glaring in big white lights.

Sometimes others can see

And take inventory.

Do not distress

Becoming a better me,

A better you,

All about changing habits

Changing attitudes,

Redefining yourself,

Despite what others think.

The hardest work we will ever do

Glaring foibles,

Misguided missteps.

Mistakes bring clarity

Let them go.

Teaches resilience

In the face of disaster.

Lessons we did not need

To encounter.

Ability to look beyond,

Step out of our own way,

Allow change to be the compass

Find a new direction.

~STEP ASIDE~

Stick your toe out

Get right to it.

Somebody gonna step on your shoes

Try to remove the shine,

Because your shoes are bright,

Never dimmed by the darkness.

Light flickers

From the tops

Casting shadows

As you go.

Let them try

Each day you gonna shine,

Buff those shoes

Gleaming all bright.

Let them shine.

Stick your whole foot out

First the right,

Then the left,

Do the two-step

All alone.

Cuz you gonna learn

To step aside

As the naysayers go

Their shoes are dim,

Cuz they do not spit shine

Their own shoes,

Nor make the effort

To stick their toes out.

~HEAVENLY PIVOT~

Rearrange,

Repaint,

Season of understanding

Season of light,

Being and becoming are one in the same.

I shift from looking out

To looking in,

Mythology of my singular life

Reminds me of who I am

Who I am meant to be.

My heart flutters

With each experience

I had to let go.

Lifetime of learning,

Lifetime of loving,

Lifetime of losing,

Lifetime of moving on.

Without exception I feel…

Pangs of loss

Pangs of what could not happen

Pangs of what would never happen

Pangs of fright.

I learn value from loss

I learn how to let things go.

Traces of what I love

Traces of what I lost

Holding on,

Letting go.

Meet each day

As a new horizon

A sanctuary

A heavenly pivot.

Vitality,

Aliveness,

As I continue to learn.

ON WRITING

~LINGERS~

When my writing lingers

Peripheral vision standing still

To write when inspired

Letting my character lead the way

She always shows me

What she wants me to say.

A treasury of inspired ideas flows to me in divinely guided ways.

~WRITER~

A writer writes

Sometimes lagging in between

To catch her breath

To imagine the unseen.

~STORY~

Writing is pulling a story

From your soul

Story to paper

Allowing your imagination

To freely flow

Into a story only you know.

Into a story only you can tell.

When I am fully present all possibilities assemble.

~SCRIBBLE~

I may be working a regular job

But I am thinking about writing my book.

So many ideas to scribe,

My character is waiting

She knows she is a hobby

And she does not pay the bills.

So off she lets me

When I return home,

She greets me with expectation

Tapping me gently on the back.

We have a story to tell

Sit together

Enjoy a hot tea

One letter, one word, one story at a time.

~ASK MYSELF~

I ask myself

Why poetry matters

Write only when

Spirit gathers.

Memorable feelings

Emotions

Thoughts that shatter.

Relevant heart

Soulful chatter

Make it resonate

Subject matter.

We can all relate

A story to reflect

No need to impersonate.

My life

Your life

Personified

Each line

From it take,

A story of me

A life not by mistake.

We search together

Words to make sense

Valleys of heartache

Wrenching battles.

Dust off the billows

Continue...

To the next

Line of transgression

Our best intentions.

Good flows in,
creativity flows out.

~I CAN WRITE A STORY~

I can write a story

With my prose

For shits and giggles

To amuse

Or oppose.

Make you squirm

Uncomfortable,

In the minute.

Thought provoking,

Inspiring,

But all the while

You think,

Ponder on yourself

All that makes you tick

All that makes you sick

All that makes you smile.

So here I go,

Writing in dismay

What comes next

Never to betray,

Mindless matter

Mindless chatter

I never know

How much to give away.

~MUSES~

Muses keep me busy

Inspiration by the minute

Scribing thoughts

Collecting 'sprickets'.

Who would have 'thunk'

Charming soulful ways

Bored into my memory

Write more, they say.

Get it out there

More to follow

We are present

When you listen

We speak the way.

A fellow writer

Glorious poet

Workmate and friend

They may not know

A singular word

Ignites my soul

Get to it.

Memories are muses

Touching my fate

Of backwards and forwards

To scribe a clean slate.

To follow and leave

Perish the past

Muses, they guide my folly

Into the ether.

On your travels of self-discovery,
plant memories to feed your soul
and blossoms for harvest.

~FICTION~

I write fiction

Each story

Fiction of me

Fiction of my imagination,

Soon

Fiction of my memories.

Fiction gives me permission

To write without omission

Truth and untruth

I can make believe,

Each line of text

Plot what comes next.

My fiction has no limit

Censorship or critique

Fiction incarnate,

Fiction mystique.

~WHISPERS IN THE WIND~

Whispers they chatter

Stories to share

Long forgotten memories

Asking me to tell.

Share the stories

Each one new

Rendition of a life

Waiting on the tale.

Stories worth telling

Stories worthy of share

Each story a whisper

Gently tugging at my ear.

Compelling me to write

A song so deep

Creeps from crevices

Secrets no longer to keep.

Stories that matter

Touching your heart

No longer the distance

Ready to start.

Whispers in the wind

Ready to carry

A lifetime,

A legacy,

Struggles worth sharing.

SHOULDA COULDA WOULDA

~BEST CHOICE, WRONG DECISION~

Dad was right

Should have listened,

Mike was the best choice

I made the wrong decision.

Best friends for life

I see it so clearly now,

He married another

I lost out, somehow.

Right in front of me

All that time

We were young

Learning our way,

I let him pass by

I let him get away.

Here we are

Forty-five years on

He is happily married

I am still alone.

So, kick me up the backside

I messed up

Threw away my best friend

A major mistake.

Still today

Remaining best friends

What could have been

Will never come again.

~DETOURS~

Distractions and detours

Metaphysics for my life,

Theory based on time and reality

Because plan A became plan C.

Everything changes and life is never ,

What I thought it would be.

A higher power had better detours

And distractions merely a metaphor.

I never meant to look back

Or even consider

What was.

The 'was' part of my life

Extinct.

As moments changed to a lifetime

Detours to destination

Ended up in one direction,

Final destination,

Still unknown.

Someone took my hand

Showed me

A future of metaphors,

Of possibilities,

A shifting reality

Better than my ideas.

Your journey is your story. Write a good one.

Your journey is your story. Write a good one.

Your journey is your story. Write a good one.

Your journey is your story. Write a good one.

Your journey is your story. Write a good one.

Your journey is your story. Write a good one.

~MORE OR LESS~

The more I did more

The more you did less.

An uphill battle

Decided to call it quits.

Felt like eternity

Getting out with all my wits,

Suffocating in his unwillingness

To try any harder.

As if minimum was enough,

Just enough to get by,

The ache and struggle

Living without desire.

As if desiring more

Was a sin

Just doing essentials

Does not require more effort.

To subdue what you do not have

If you are comfortable in the margins

Getting by is enough.

Not expecting yourself to get better

No desire to improve.

Using God and religion as an excuse

Your next life will not be any different.

No motivation to get it right

In the here and now.

Your excuses will follow

And remain unchanged,

Because you did not make an effort

Doing less was the easiest excuse.

Ten years later

Rebuilt with more

Each passing day

Living with desire

Leaving was the only answer.

Living in the margins was not my calling

I could never subscribe,

Living in your thoughtless margins.

Would never give up

Despite your never efforts

The more I do now

The more I grow

Just had to set myself free.

In every day, in every way, choose your joy.
Joy is the magic ingredient that lights our souls
and shelters us with promise and potential.

~PERPETUATING~

At most

Six or seven

Too young to feel

Unlovable and unlikable.

To think a parent

Guardian of one so young

Would allow family

To abuse

Then condone

Reinforcing the message

A child all alone.

To sort through the messages

Never understanding

Adults full of spite

Dispensing their vective

Misappropriating their hate.

A defenseless child

Becomes defensive

Fighting back

Never to escape.

A mother's extended family

Vipers and small minded

Afraid of the small

Guileless child

That has their number.

And calls them out

Because she doesn't deserve

Hate-filled messages

Designed to shame

Keeping her small.

Abusive adults

Who spew their evil

They work in gangs.

A cycle of sickness

Spurious words

Designed to cripple.

So she grows up not understanding

And believing the untrue

Striving to be loved

And choosing a shrew.

To perpetuate false messages

Unconscious beliefs

Dispelling the myths

A lifetime to sort

False doctrine

Believed to be true.

A child unlovable

A child unlikable

At six or seven

How cruel.

~STORM~

You went through a shit storm

Felt like eternity

Raging against you.

Now you are back

A stronger version

A weathered veteran

No matter the debris

Whirling about.

You trudged forward

Knowing it would end

You have been there

You know how to get through

Calm the storm,

Subdue the wind.

You have the right attitude

You know it will pass

Your constant companion

Has your back.

Even on your knees

Crawling

All fours got you there.

~WHAT YOU SAID~

What you said

Yes, that

Meant to cause harm

Inflict pain.

My soul to dread

Your heinous words

Thrashing out

Can't hold your tongue

Gotta let it out.

Hate-filled

Your words

Cut and slice

Sharp and direct

How awful to project

That hate upon another.

You must feel

That way about yourself

Now the truth

Comes out.

What you say

Has nothing to do with me.

Turn your words

In the right direction

Not towards me.

Tell your story

All about you

Instead of sending

Vile and spite.

I am not crazy

I do not imagine

Your diatribe

Describing you

And hate for yourself

All comes blubbering out.

I won't take it personal

No, I won't listen

Your mirror

Shines a light

Into the dark

Crevices

Of your soul.

Everyone can see

The shallowness

Lack of control.

So, take your verbiage

Does not belong to me,

Garbage you sputter

Rubbish, that is all you speak.

No goodness utters

From a soul

Blackened

From disease.

~**WHEN**~

When did you start

Doing less

And I compensated,

With more?

Was it always like that?

Did I just choose to ignore?

Told myself

You would step up

You would do more.

Until eventually

Came and went.

Hundreds of times over

Time

To relent.

Years upon years

I accepted less.

I continued to do more,

With your less.

You sucked all the energy,

Never wanting to step up,

Content with your less

And me

With my more.

~TRUTH~

I know the truth

Cuz you just can't listen

Detriment to your lesson.

You just can't believe

You might have it wrong

You know in your head

You were right all along.

But, you got to poke

Keep the knife sharp

The edges of the blade

Meant to do harm.

This point to prove

You need to be right

Blind to your blind spots

Fractures your mind.

I helped when you were down

Now you retract all the goodness

Because you cannot accept

What someone else blesses.

So, it does not matter

Anymore.

You destroyed all the goodwill

Your love so shallow

As with all your friendships

Spurious vective

Destroying what you cannot accept

As good

And you become...

Reckless.

~KARMA~

Karma,

Uniquely yours

What you get in return

Floating out there

Waiting your turn.

Karma omniscient

Meant just for you.

If you have done wrong

Karma

Eventually

Returns

Just for you.

Be careful what you do wrong,

Unto another

As you sow seeds of

Belligerence

Jealousy

Lies

Untruth.

Turning it around

Making another the bad guy

As you rationalize your deceit,

Triangulate your wrongdoing,

Backup from family and friends

Help you walk away,

Gingerly

Out of your score to keep.

Eventually you will wonder

Why this is happening to you

As if innocence

Was not something new.

Don't bother coming

Back around for help

I've held you up

A lifetime of guilt.

You've done wrong.

Twist the truth

To suit your ends

Always someone else's fault

You never win.

Take your karma

Don't push it to the side

That shit is meant

Just for you,

Take it in stride.

Uniquely fit.

Your transgressions

To apply

Karma always gets you

Feel your guts churn

Deep, deeper

Inside.

~I SEE YOU~

I see you

Resplendent in your finery

All duded out

Part of the scenery.

Something special

Not to ignore

Center of attention

Yes, an attention whore.

Catch yourself on

You aren't that unique

You think all girls want you

Center of mystique.

Your rings and your baubles

Money galore

But you're bald and elderly.

Magic blue pills

They make you feel better

To feel more alive

You date 20 years younger.

Always seeking the prize

Using and abusing,

To fit your lifestyle.

Gals my age don't want you

Date your own range

Do yourself a favor

You don't deserve anything better.

~GOT TO GO~

My life started

Long before you arrived

My life will continue

Right after you leave

To the curb...

You go

You go.

Not soon enough

Waste of my time

Thinking you are

The only one

Who can strike

My chime.

Soon to learn

Sisters won't tolerate your kind.

So, into yourself

You're out of line.

Mister, you and your charm

Self-glorifying

Yes, the harbinger kind.

Foreshadowing demise

Your disguise.

Sisters see through it

Cuz guys like you

A dime a minute.

Sisters know,

Sisters know,

You got to go,

You got to go.

~FAVOR~

I did myself a favor

Let you go

Not in this lifetime

Together, not meant to roam.

Stars won't twinkle

Stars won't shine

Our paths divergent

Not meant to pass.

You go your way

I'll go mine,

No need to stop

Or linger,

I will travel solo

Leaving you behind.

~HEARD~

I have heard

Enough of what I should be

Enough of what I need to be

Need to be and should be

No longer need to be part

Of my should.

Distracting words

Cause anxiety and stress

To measure up

To another's idea of success.

Defining words

Meant to control

Coerce and erase,

Individual identity.

Dislocating the me

From myself.

Please take your should be's,

Your need be's,

And shove them up your

Never to be's.

~PROBABLY LIKELY POSSIBLY~

Three adverbs

Sitting by the wayside

Unable to make up their minds.

On the fence is easiest place to sit

Not let anyone down

Not make a choice.

No and yes are too definitive.

Leave it open,

Let it breathe,

Verbs take action

Better to 'ly'.

Leaving me hanging

While you straddle the fence

One leg over,

One leg hence.

A conversation built on potential

Likely later,

Possibly whence,

Probably never.

~PRECIOUS WOUND~

Never far from my memory

Burned into my brain

Seared onto my heart

You left me

On the road to transformation.

Ruin and debris

Cast about my feet

Leaving a trail of destruction

Memories lost

Memories found

Disparaged parts of me

Strewn about the ground.

Precious memories

Precious wounds

I let you drift

I let you go

My road of destruction

Became my road to redemption.

Thoughts that did not serve me

Memories that reminded me

A dirge of a path

Mournful song

Exile on an island of my own.

Precious island

Precious wound

Precious path

Until I learned

To make new memories my home.

I felt alone

In my sanctified way

Took the journey by myself

My metaphysical landscape

A shift into the unknown.

My wounds to recover

All that gravity can deprive

As I sit in wonder

Reconstructing me

One day at a time.

      (Inspiration from "Eat Pray Love",

        Elizabeth Gilbert)

GRATITUDE AND SPIRIT

~THE GOD I KNOW~

God moves mightily in my life

Amazes me,

Shows me better ways and better days.

He showers me with kindness

Shelters me with His wings

Protects me from myself.

Each day I follow His inspired messages

And feel His infinite love.

Even in this vast universe,

He knows me.

I lean into Him for guidance

As He guides with wisdom

I have yet to comprehend.

Always in the right direction

Gently nudging with His hand.

~TRIO~

Simple request

Draw closer to God

Feel His closeness

His love never waivers.

A forever promise

No matter my mistakes

He takes me in

Lets me falter

Question His grace.

I always return

To His warm embrace.

A fondness

A devotion

Just for me

One of His many.

He always sees

My frailties

My shortcomings

He takes up the slack

Secures my well-being.

The trio

Father, Son, Holy Ghost

Remind me of comfort, grace and humility

Their love extended

Meant for me.

The great I AM

Savior and Holy Ghost

Miracle workers

At my behest.

Know me by name

What makes me tick

All my quirks

My foibles.

Yet here I portend

To understand

All the Godly love

They extend.

A human condition

Only the trio understands.

I
allow
fun
and
laughter
to
brighten
and
lighten
my
way.

~GRATITUDE~

Gratitude is my attitude

Daily compass to guide the way

First thought each morning

Last thought end of day.

~GRATITUDE TODAY~

Gratitude for the big things

Gratitude for the little things

Giving thanks for all I have

Giving thanks for all I see

Giving thanks in preparation

For what I am about to receive.

Simple to express

Simple to explain

Gratitude in my heart

Means I never complain.

Always on the bright side

Sunshine even rain

Giving thanks is extraordinary

Only the humble maintain.

The right to graciousness

Found in my heart

Easily grows there

With each positive thought.

Giving thanks is simple

Gratitude for what is lost

Gratitude for what is found

You will always find me

Where gratitude abounds.

As I trust in a higher power and relinquish control of outcomes, I become a channel for better – beyond my wildest dreams.

~BLESSES~

Tune in

Turn that dial

To the frequency of

Gratitude

Lights your smile.

Each morning give thanks

Start your day

Praying to remember

Praying to give meaning

Your soul's delay.

Listen for signs

Silently spoken

Centered and quiet

Aligned, unbroken.

Gratitude to brighten

The only way

You tuned in

You listened

Recognized what was given.

~HEALING~

Healing begins with feeling

Forced deep inside

Buried

Ancient memory

Perhaps shame or old desire

Not meant for my tomorrow.

Push it further down

Hope it goes away

Then a dream

Ignites the fire.

Forces me to remember

What I once desired.

Outcome not to encourage

Pain and discomfort

Tasting the bile

Of my desire.

Stuck in my throat

Reminds me of the pain I sought to absolve

Still here

All the while.

A constant companion

Colors my lenses

In all of my interactions

In all of my lessons.

Deal with the shame, hurt and guilt.

Treat them as friends

Gentle yet alert.

Older me can heal

The little girl me

Who did nothing wrong

But bury her hurt.

Love her pain

Love her shame.

But, most of all...

Help her love...

Herself again.

~SOURCE~

Source

Lights my way

Illuminates each step

Firmly grips my hand

Guides and protects.

In tune with direction

I quiet my mind

Listen

Solitude for a few moments

Each morning

Each night

I place concerns in a basket

Let them sit overnight.

Only Source can heal

I trust the divine

My guide for life.

Showers with goodness

Shows me better

Leads me to my very best

We work together.

Wrong to right.

Makes any struggle seem light

Carries my burdens

In Her stride.

A sense of relief each day

As I begin

Renewed by Source

Powerful friend

Knowing better is here

Each moment

Each day

Transformation

A better version of myself.

~RESIDE~

Yes, it is slippery out there

All alone

Doing this life on my own.

But, who better to catch me?

When I slip and slide

Then God who has my back

His arm to reside.

He caught me just in time

Even after a fall

His hands were ready

To pick me back up

And help me stand tall.

~BLANKET~

Bought a blanket at Costco

Softest blanket on earth

Fondly refer to it

As God's blanket.

Curl up all nice and snug

Up to my shoulders

Like a bug in a rug.

So comforting and warm

I imagine it must be

Like God's arms

Wrapped around me.

Just want to stay here

Not budge an inch

Cats won't leave my side

They like it too.

Fabric of God's blanket

Lots of room

Envelopes us in softness

Purring in accord

Let's stay in bed together

Praise God and his warmth.

Nothing is
by chance.
Serendipitous
moments are
meant just for
you.

~**ME**~

Every particle of God

Created me.

Resides in every fibre

Even in me.

Miraculous in every way

Imperfect me.

~CONVERSATIONS WITH GOD~

If I scream loud

Will He hear me?

If I cry more

Will He heal me?

If I forget He is there

Will He still know me?

If I push Him away

Will He save me?

If He is not real

Will He listen?

~PARABLE~

Sharing my oil

Does not cost much

Helping another

Who was foolish

More than enough.

If we share together

Even one lamp will do

To guide our journey.

Preparedness

Not separateness

Keeps us Holy.

Let me shine my light

Let me share my oil

Let my lamp guide

Together

More than plenty.

An ancient parable

Meeting our Maker

Two lost souls

Unprepared

Helping one another.

In the end

We stand alone.

The light we shared

Helped us

Make it home.

~FORGIVENESS~

Forgiveness

Meant for me

To let it go

Live happily.

No harm to inflict

No karma to incur

Just simple resolution

Like the flip of a switch.

Moving forward

No reason to reflect

The pain I felt

In retrospect.

God's mercy and patience

On me bestowed

Showed me the way

To act in kind

The parts so broken

I left behind.

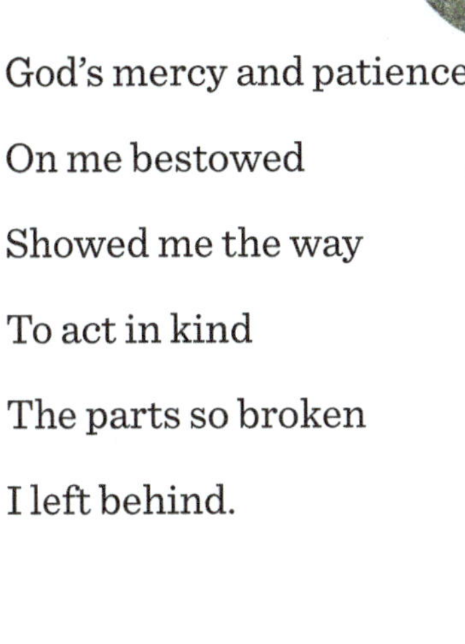

Forgiving myself

First to align

With His purpose

A love divine.

He showers me daily

Showing me the light

So bright He shines

And by His hand

 He guides me.

Forgiveness with a gaze

I linger no longer

On pain which made me stronger.

~BLISS~

I hear the morning

Bliss.

If only to continue

Throughout my day

Steadfast.

Quiet solitude

Guards my mind

Keeps me Holy

Divine.

These moments

Stillness

I pray.

God give me bliss

Throughout my day.

Blessings are God's sprinkles of joy guiding our lives. Each new day is an opportunity to participate with God and recognize you are the active ingredient.

~ALL THE THINGS~

I am grateful

All the little things

All the big things

All things in between.

But gratitude is best

When shared and spoken to others

In little ways

In big ways

And all ways in between.

Shown in the little things

In the big things

And shown in all ways in between.

A nod of understanding

A word of appreciation

A gaze of comfort

A smile to lighten the load.

All things matter when giving in earnest

The simplest of gratitude

The simplest of gestures.

~WALK IN THE LIGHT~

He lights my path

Each step I take

Encourages me forward

In loving ways.

Nudges with kindness

Sends angels

As friends.

Always remembers

My vulnerable heart.

Rescues when needed

Sometimes, taking His time.

I am divinely guided and supported.
I am grounded in the knowledge
guides and angels accompany me on
this journey. I need only ask and my
guides answer.

~FIRM IN MY FAITH~

The world wants you to believe

You need more than God

To meet your needs.

Hush, hush, hush

Background noise

The world is not the voice of discernment,

The world does not serve as a source of light.

Place your trust in Him

Walk in faith

Be of faith.

Trust in the light.

~EFFORT~

Daily effort

A simple kneel

Reminds me to be grateful

Give thanks

And listen

To His gentle heed.

Conversations with God

He knows my concerns

And needs

Heartfelt

Humble

My daily connection

To something real.

Faith

Useless without action

Faith

A promise to do

Breathes air

Into my effort.

The power of my faith

The power of my prayers

As I kneel

As I know

His promises

He delivers.

~TRUST THE AUTHOR~

Trust the Author

Invisible ink

Writes my story

Somehow knows

Beginning and end.

While I try to control

The flow of the pen

The story unfolds

Edited and deleted

Scratch outs along the way.

If I allow the author

To do His work

He writes my story

In a different way

Better than imagined.

~RENOVATING MY SOUL~

Renovating my soul

Unsettling

Unnerving

Duo of do overs and do 'agains'.

I am based on a true story

Walking into the unknown

Familiar with darkness

Searching alone

Yes, I am my own hero

Most of the time.

Until my guardian angels

Wake me from solitary solitude

And remind me

Everything I long for

Everything I need

Is made better

Is made whole

When I listen.

Stand in the gap of unknown

When invisible realm

Becomes visible realm

And then I am humbled

All the should's and ought to's

Never to pay heed

My true story

My own hero

Finds me on the journey

Never looking back.

~I TRUST~

I trust His timing

His will and His way,

God interrupts my thoughts

Reminds me that the battle is not mine

Only His.

So I believe in His timing

Divine messages

Directed to me

For me.

Creates impetus

To remember

To understand divine

Intervention

Sustains my faith

And glorifies

His plan.

INTIMACY

~LOVE LETTERS~

All the letters

I want to read

Pull to my heart

Imbue in my eyes.

Effortless words

Sung just for me

Written in your hand

Spoken with your lips.

Sweet words of endearing love

Kindest words of truest devotion

Tender words of ethereal perfection

Simple words of inexplicable heaven.

Sharing your love

On a few pages

Forever spoken

To my soul.

~LOVED~

I want to be loved

To be adored

To feel the consuming comfort

An engulfing passion.

To be touched and secured in his gaze

His gaze only for me

His hands only for my face

His lips attached to mine.

His embrace on my waist

His words grasping my heart

As he whispers

Love onto my neck

And kisses my grateful tears

Away with his warmth.

~WHISPER~

He whispers

On my neck

Lips collide

Trembling

As his mouth moves

Slowly

Into the nape

He caught my gasp

Just as I exhaled.

~EMBRACE~

Embrace me

Make me all warm

Fill up my insides

Safe from storms.

Shelter my body

Wind and rain

You got me

Safe from life's billows

Blustering

Insane.

Kiss to my forehead

A sign complete

Gestures of comfort

Protected and secure.

In your space

I can relax

Trusting in your

Shadow

You won't let me go

Until I am ready

To face it on my own.

~BREASTS~

He likes the back

The breast

And all the rest.

But, boobs

His favorite.

Meant for his kisses

Meant for his face

Nestle in there

He feels safe.

Soft and gentle

His caresses all over

Her Godly breasts.

Reverance not folly

Meant for pleasure

She gladly succumbs

His kisses forever.

~LIPS~

Your kisses

Devour me whole

Claim my essence

Engulf my mouth

Ah...

To feel your warmth.

Tingles spread

Warmth glides

To all the right places

Fulfilling my need

I cry and plead.

As your kisses

Gently unfold

Down my neck

Hands gather

All the rest.

Bits of heaven

At your behest.

Surrender

No control

Thunderous harsh breathing

Wake of desire.

More kisses

Tongue to inspire

Lips of soft figs

Travel my shoulders

Trailing of tongue

Down my spine.

Your kisses

All consuming

Light my fire

Find my insane.

~BACKSEAT~

Backset of your car

Never so fun

You thought it was for car seats and groceries

Only to learn...

Stretch your legs above your head

Head rests for feet

There you go

Getting after it.

Laughing all the while

Knowing a cop gonna catch you

Inflagratto.

Half the excitement

Hoping to not get stuck

You thought you only did this shit

In your youth

More fun as an adult.

FAMILY

~HOME~

All I need

To hear my father's voice

Go home to mother

Sunday, a special place.

Sacred breakfast

Mother cooking

We sit around the table

Enjoying the taste of homemade.

With my parents

All to our own

Nobody on the phone

Just us together

Time alone.

A table of love

Voices familiar

Kids have come home

Grandkids enjoy

Grandma and Grandpa

Not here for long.

Their voices will carry

Imbued in their memory

A time so precious

Around for breakfast

In my parents' home.

~GRANDPA~

He sits to pee

Instead of standing

'Cuz the splash

Hits him in the knees.

Grandma nags him into submission

He is a man

Can pee on his own

Without her direction.

No need to worry 'bout the lid

Up or down

Down it sits

So grandma doesn't fall in.

No cause to worry

Middle of the night

No cold porcelain

Grips her behind.

The seat is down

Greets her bottom.

Grandpa obliges

To keep the peace

He likes his meals

Without conversation.

At least for today

He knows he's done good

Cleans up after himself

No tracks in his shorts

Or on the porcelain.

Grandma taught him

Especially when he was drinkin'

To sit and behave

Without all the fussin'.

If your radar (intuition) goes off around a certain person or group of people, leave. Your guidance system is telling you the situation is unhealthy and harmful. Especially with people who give you the creeps or you just intuitively distrust the person – stay away. This isn't projection – this is protection.

~HOW TO RAISE YOUR PARENTS~

An adult child

Teaching her parents

How to communicate

And let her grow.

Raising your parents

They need to acknowledge

They did their job right

To let you go.

Young parents

Starting early

They grew up

Raising you right.

The only way they could

The only way they knew.

Now they are older

Hitting their prime

Retirement years around the corner

Still worried about their child.

A family of your own

No time to look out

For your aging parents

You are raising yours right.

They taught you well

Your push and pull

Can be confusing,

Still needing your parents

And they need you.

Let them grow up

To be on their own

Time away

You are on your own.

Release the strings

That keep you attached

You will sometimes need mommy

That is a fact.

You raised your parents

You did it right

Adulting can be hard

They taught you well

Their roles never retire.

~ONE WORD~

Only one word makes my day...

The sound of wee voices

Calling from afar.

Little feet

Little hands

Grabbing for grandma

Toes in the sand.

Down the slide

A bit more coaxing

A gentle push

On the swing

Giggles abound.

Swimming together

Playing Godzilla and Lochness

Daring to jump farther

Splashing in the laughter.

The call to grandma

Watch this!

Watch me!

The most important sound

Because when you are grandma

Spoil them rotten

Time together

Never forgotten.

~GRANNY PANTIES~

I wear granny panties

Yes I do.

Old lady nightgowns

Like grandma used to.

First thing after work

Bra thrown askew

My girls are free at last

Sagging too.

Never thought

I'd reach the age

I don't care a wit

If you aren't amazed.

By my timeless beauty

No room to condemn.

Thighs rub together

It ain't no sin.

Cellulite to discover

Never far from view

Each year in passing

An extra pound or two.

Hell yes I'm aging

All in stride

One hot grandma

A cougar inside.

~SISTERS~

We may quarrel and squabble

Years ignoring each other

But don't misunderstand us

We got the courage

To fight.

Every insurrection

Our lifetime together

Never let it go.

Cut that vindictiveness,

Remove from our souls.

Four girls

Mother chose a favorite.

Not protected

Extended family dysfunction.

Mother did not have the courage

To defend her young.

Troubled memories

Followed individual paths.

We chose the same type of man

Same type of lessons

Same 'ol shenanigans.

Gluttons for punishment

We shared the mess

Each single after a lifetime

Still trying our best.

Making better choices

All on our own.

Sad to think

We still squabble

Argue and share

Two-faced reckoning

Making one sister the bad guy

Taking sides.

Deliberately misunderstanding

Because we have not learned

Compassionate understanding.

We see one another

In each other's mistakes.

Makes our memories less awful

When we blame and tear asunder.

Facing ourselves

Facing our mistakes

Facing each other

We have to make recompence,

We have to make amends.

Sisters, we are the same.

Sisters, we are one.

*Forgiveness
is no longer
giving energy
and attention
to underserving
situations and
people.*

~OLDEST SISTER~

Oldest sister

Leader of the pack

You will never replace her

That is her status.

Looks after younger

Siblings in the ranks

A calling just for her

She knows her place.

Parents often rely

On her steadfast pace

While still a child

She learns grace.

Accepts her calling

Without a voice

Does what she is told

Has no choice.

Parents beware

She is only a child

Not your right hand

Not your folly.

Do not subscribe her

To your lack of ability

Step up

And be the parent.

Older sister

You hold my hand

When crossing the street

You give me baths

Warm my feet.

Tuck me in at night

Read me books.

Into adulthood

Forever my oldest sister

Still in your role

Leader of me.

Always looking up

To my sister, my savior

Separate from the others

Never obsolete.

Still, you hold my hand

Comfort in my dreams.

Older sister

In each of our lifetimes

Heavenly sent

Together we will be.

SURVIVAL GUIDE FOR GROWTH

~NEED~

Anxious anxiety

Keeping me from here and now

Stealing my present

Pretending I am here.

Fearful fretting

Bars of darkness

Steal my sight

Impeding my vision.

Controlling climate

To make everything perfect

To bend to my will

Instead of being willing.

Desperately desperate

Hard to surrender

To a will not my own

Trusting in another

Trusting the unknown.

Perpetuating present

Daily reminder

Practice the OM

Prayer for my need to control

Prayer for my need to let go.

~FALLING APART~

Only when falling apart

Can I pick up the broken bits

And make new

An imperfect version

Made better.

Breaking into pieces

I can reconstruct

And rearrange

Glue everything together

Sauder into place

Choose new colors

Reflect and replace

A rough draft.

Lots of edits

Falling apart

Shards of broken

Loving each bit

Ruptured

Still working

On my masterpiece.

A true friend is a friend all of the time,

not just part of the time.

~IF I COULD NOT FAIL~

As I fail towards success

And discover lost tragedies

I realize my journey

Was meant to create more memories.

Success and failure

Inevitable at last

Means finding my way

Along a non-trodden path.

Failure is just an expletive

Success an outcome

We derive their meaning

From our wis-dom.

To fail is to succeed

A mindset of possibilities

Along the path to failure

Is desire to be.

~WOULD IT BE ANY DIFFERENT?~

Would it be any different

If I were someplace different?

I wished to be here

And now I am restless

Thinking of another place

Other than here.

That is the danger

Of being content

Of arriving at a destination

Once intended.

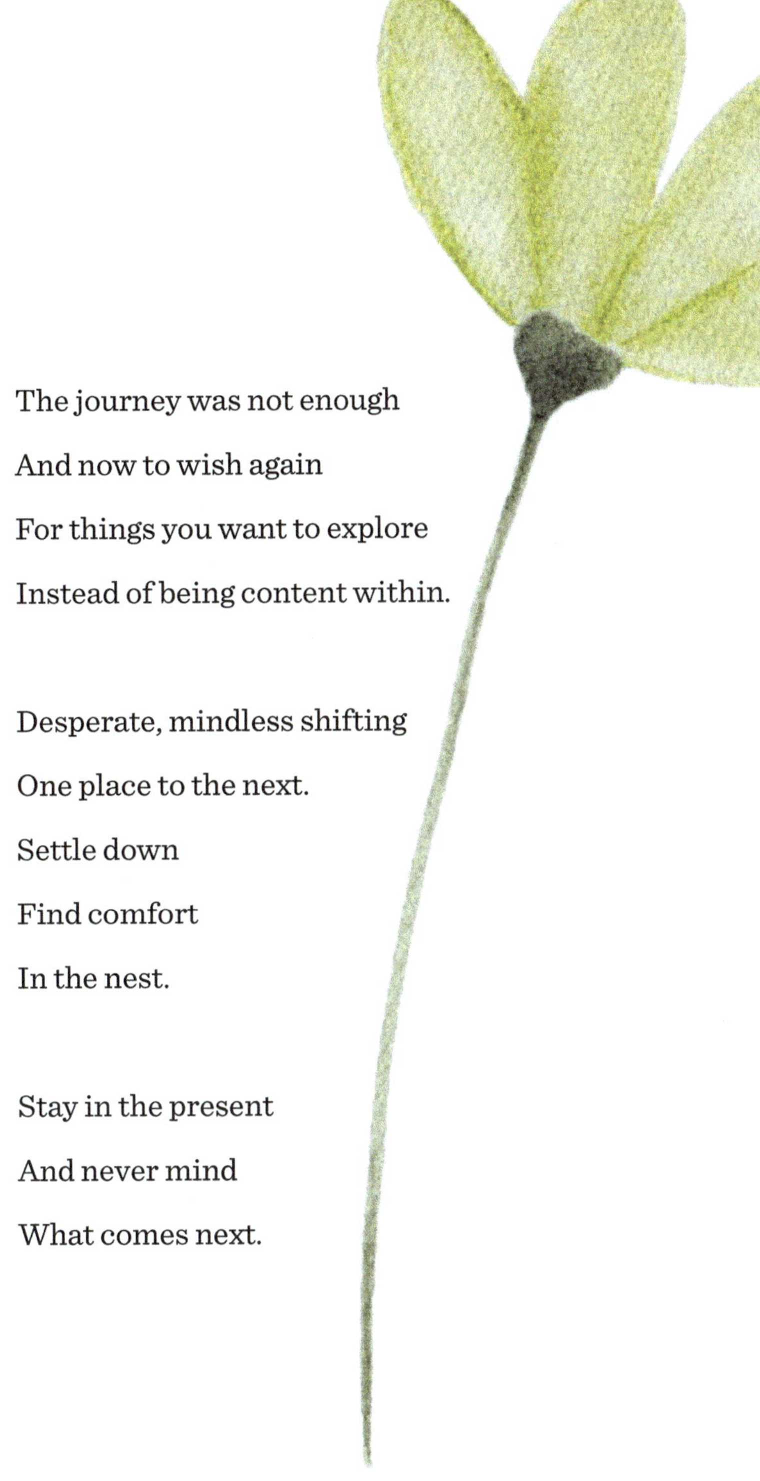

The journey was not enough

And now to wish again

For things you want to explore

Instead of being content within.

Desperate, mindless shifting

One place to the next.

Settle down

Find comfort

In the nest.

Stay in the present

And never mind

What comes next.

~HUMILITY~

When you get it wrong

Admit it quickly

Apologize

Move past the blunder.

Offense not taken

When quick to recognize

Error in judgment

Lessons

Meant to push forward.

Sorry, such a simple word

Changed behavior

Indicates resolve

Get it right next time

Plenty of next times to come.

Humble yourself

Knowing not always right

Hey, I got this wrong

Maybe next time

I will get it right.

Each humbling experience

An arrow to your quiver

At least you tried

At least you apologized

And moved beyond.

I am big enough to

Admit my blunders

Admit my faulty words

Admit I can do better

For myself

For my personal resolve.

No pride or ego here

To ruin my growth

I learned long ago

If I step on shoes

At least leave the shine

Polish my etiquette

Humble my toes.

Not the last time

Blunders aplenty

Humility is my ally

Got lots of practice

A bigger person

Changes

That is all that matters.

~IRRELEVANT~

When feeling irrelevant

Nobody seems to care

Mired in self-pity

Despair.

Pick yourself up girl

Nobody cares

You are your own savior

And God got you here.

Feelings are temporary

Give thoughts no matter

You got this girl

Stand up to your despair.

Each moment

Just a breath

Blow it out.

Inhale what is left

Give thanks for the lesson

May not be your time

A season of quiet

Reminding you to sit still

Allow 'you' to renew.

Comparison is unjust

No mercy in envy

The grace you need

You must embrace

On your own

You got this girl.

Your worth is not a transactional exchange or based on value. Your worth is a loving relationship between you and you. Only you determine your value and set appropriate definitions and boundaries.

~SOLO~

A traveler

Chose a distant path

Soul assignment

Meant for one

Legs dredge through quicksand.

Feet drag along

This karmic jokester

Mentioned adventure

Yet here I am

Fighting an illusion

Of progress.

And when I arrive

Destination savvy

Time to do it again

My karmic justice

Treading water

Climbing that rocky trail

And still I wander

My solo path.

~SOMETHING~

Something has changed

In my core

Incessant drive

More and more.

Needless wanting

Driven

Just me and my desires

Never in one place for long.

~THROTTLE~

Full throttle

Gotta meet the next goal

Never-ending metrics

Stealing my soul.

Keep up with expectations

Taking a toll

Mental reserves

Always on the go

Auto pilot.

I have joined the masses

Big or small

I have done it all

Serving a digital master.

Time to stop

Catch my breath

So many years on the go

If only for a moment

Reflect.

Why I keep on

Serving another

No time for self.

Too busy working

To notice the noise

Just to catch my breath

I silently break.

Wondering why I continue

This never-ending race

My humanity

Abandoning

Grace.

~CAN~

You probably can

Just don't know it,

Dip your foot into the water

Get down to it.

A first step

A stumble

You get used to it,

Until finally

Your can...

Can do it.

When our thoughts, emotions and actions are fully aligned, purpose and meaning for our life are the resounding outcomes. Our soul evolves as we create a sacred agreement with purpose. We find deeper meaning with each new experience.

~LET IT GO~

Let it go

Let it be

Surrender control

Breathe – Release – Relax - Believe.

Leave space

For the unseen.

Trust in better

Expect to let go

Expect to let it be.

Good only gets better

When you release control.

~OPEN DOOR~

A door once opened

So you imagined

Led you here

You went on a tangent.

Unsupervised

This was not your door

To open.

A door once closed

Is now open

The time is right

To make it happen,

Swing it wide

Peer inside.

All this meant for you

You took your time.

Discovered the right door

Or let it happen

Timing was right

No need to force.

All you can fathom

Left room for the unexpected

Behind the right door

Your blessings await

All restored.

~PUT IT DOWN~

Put it down

No need to carry

All on your own

Your journey

Meant to be light.

Burden of

Yester-year

Yester-life

Not meant to travel

Into today

Into tonight.

Now you can travel

Into today

Into tonight

Shoulders free

Hands light

Mind unburdened

Into today

Into tonight.

~STARTING OVER~

Starting over

Not so bad

A second chance

Start anew

Build a life

Uniquely you.

No matter your age

You can do it

One step

One day

Each minute

Put your shoulder...

To it.

Press forward

No matter the muck

Up to your chin

Trudge, trudge, trudge

Through it.

Some days are down

Some days are up

Head in the right direction

Set your compass.

All up to you now

Nobody to blame.

Courage

Not to falter

Not to shame.

Friends to help

Guide your way

Sage advice

Listen

Listen

Your heart will guide

Your legs will lead

Your head will not falter.

It gets better.

Trust in

Your guidance system

Never to waiver

You got this

Create yourself anew.

~THERAPY~

A suggestion of therapy

Once or twice

I left in search of

Good advice.

Instead, I talked and talked

Blithering away

To hear nothing but silence

My therapist did not say.

Sound of my frustrations

Must be a bore.

Challenges and woes,

Bouncing off bookshelves

Of never been told.

Same story

Different soul

My therapist

Must be haunted

So much to disclose.

Ears on fire

No discomfort shown.

Meaningless jabber

Listening to me blabber.

Deprives the room of fresh air

Of all good feelings...

Despair.

Rewinding the years

Rehashing

Not forgetting,

Strangles my progress

As my therapist stares.

Because I am unforgiving

Unforgetting

My part in the story

I am in this too

An active participant

Nothing is new.

Stop the recording.

Sage this room.

Cleanse my spirit.

Mix the smoke.

Show me how to

End this message

Rewrite the story

Move to resolution

Free myself

Participate in evolution.

Only I can make changes

Poke the spokes

Listening to my ranting

Must give my therapist mini strokes.

She really wants to tell me

What I already know

Quit your bitchin'

Nothing to despair

You need to grow some balls

To evolve and repair.

~BLUES~

Blues got me down

Turn on some music

Listen so loud

To favorite tunes

Change of mood

Real fast.

Get up

Move to the rhythm

Boogie all through

Find momentum

Feeling better

Remembering

How music makes me feel

When I let go

When I let it all go

Sing out of tune.

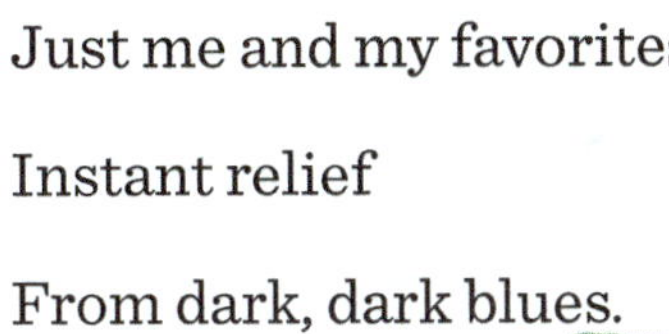

Just me and my favorites

Instant relief

From dark, dark blues.

Cuz baby

Music kicks my ass into gear

Keeps me pushing on

Keeps me feeling good

Keeps me remembering

A fire...

About to ignite

My soul.

~THE PAST~

The past does not need me

The past does not see the new me

The past knows it's place

Distant for a reason

I no longer live there.

The past does not deserve a second chance

The past does not deserve a second look

Let it go

I no longer live there.

The past no longer breathes

No life of it's own

Without my attention

Without my energy

Without my recollection.

I breathe life into my present

That is where I choose to live

Reflect on the moment

Here I live free

Of unkind reflection

Of regret.

Here I create

Here I renew my spirit

Because I left the past behind

Shut that door

Blew that popsicle stand

Long, long ago.

~NAVIGATOR~

Today

Like yesterday

And tomorrow too

I will navigate my lessons

In earnest

No matter

The hue.

Today

Like yesterday

And tomorrow too

I will navigate this life

Dream capacity

At this age

Never squandered

Hope renewed.

Eternal compass

Finding my way

Even with darkness

Light kept me straight

My eyes shuddered

Hands for shields

Feeling my way.

Tomorrow

Like today

Yesterday too

Master navigator

Compass to help

My constant view.

~TEACHER~

Pain is my teacher

Together through thick and thin

Divulging our weaknesses

Pain to teacher

Teacher to pain

We carry our lessons

Shoulders so strong

Never realizing

We never did this alone.

Each other for company

Encouraging stride for stride

Alongside each other

Our paths collide

Healing my pain

Healing my teacher

Skilled navigators

God our guide.

~VISION~

Two wolves

Appeared in the mist

As the road

I traveled

Split

Into two single lanes.

Directing me towards

Only one lane free

So, I followed.

Solitary two

Eyes glowing

In the dark.

Heavy gloom

They showed

My path

Misdirected

Misguided.

A different perspective

Towards what mattered.

Mist never lifting

Shrouded in dark.

Headlights diffused

Earth's craggy night.

Two wolves directing

As if spirit animals

Could map directions

Clear my vision

Help me find

My way.

Solitary journey

I thought

On my own

And found two companions

Meeting me halfway.

Wisdom to follow

As they split my vision

Into potential

Waiting to be explored.

~ALIVE~

When you were alive

Did you live?

Did you take breath each day

Knowing

Soon you would be dead?

Your life once happened

Did you make it count?

Do all you could?

So, you could remember,

When time has passed

Lived life with vigor.

Hey, I did this

No excuses

No remorse

I lived,

Made it worthwhile

Made a difference.

When the calling arrived

Last bit of music

Did you dance towards the light,

Knowing the next life...

Would be even better?

~BARREN~

Barren is a season

No toil

Only rest

Branches seem lonely

Time to reflect

Sap has withered

Bottom to decay

In time to renew

Spring to display.

A womb of comfort

Nurtured in its stay

Laden or empty

Arms or branches

Seasons will change

And in tiny buds

Life renewed.

What once was barren

Born anew.

Inspiration is a mixture of being open, listening, feeling and intuitively knowing the next step. Inspiration always has an action component...

~BLINDING BLIND SPOTS~

Blinding blind spots

Impervious to my knowledge

Slip from my distance

Slip from my view.

Blind to my blind spots

Never knew

Periphery has blinders

Focus askew

Still I wonder

How I got here

Simpleton

Lacking

All my keys out of tune.

Blind to my blind spots

Sun glares through my lenses

Refactors refracting

All I thought I knew

Trick of my eyes

Once I thought

But I blew it

Blind spots hiding

My distorted view.

~GRIEF~

Just make it fast

Do it quick

Help me recover

'Lickety' split.

Ignore incessant

Pain and remorse

Better things to deal with

Facing discomfort

Get it over.

Subdue the past

Make it not real

Deal with it later.

Until finally

I realize

Grief won't dissipate

Grief is a process

My feelings deserve

Better treatment

Gentle acceptance.

My human condition

One of a kind

This hole of suffering

belongs to me

As I move through grief

Pain will slowly subside.

My aching wound

Slowly recovers

I had to face this

On my own.

Dig deep inside

Uncover my hurt

Because I let it fester

Obstinate in my pain.

Touching my wounds

Helped me recover

From grief

From regret

Unspoken. pain.

~SILENCE~

Silence for my noisy head

Can be disturbing

Full of awkward seconds

Full of never been said.

Time alone

So used to my mouth moving

Never ending noise

In silence I retreat.

Shut off my brain

Hear nothing

Just my inhale and exhale

Concentrate on the rhythm

Lulling me to a place.

Draw the curtain

In silence

I do not listen

I do not see

I find myself there

Quiet and serene.

In the darkness

Black enveloping

I find bits of myself

Voices drowned out

By my noisy self.

A smaller voice asking

Too weak to speak up

To be heard

And remembered.

Only in silence

Can her voice be clear

Competing for attention

Until magic occurs.

Open to answers

Long unheard.

Solitude

Sacred moments

Sanctify

Cleanses my spirit

Opens my mind.

Only in silence

Can I make space to listen

To quiet unnecessary voices

Now unhidden.

In silence

I hear only

God's whisper to sustain

Just this moment

Bliss to remain.

I find myself here

Sacred alone

My tiny space of blackness

Peaceful

Unexposed.

Keeps me in quiet.

Noisy voices unheard

As I take time to shut off

And my world expand.

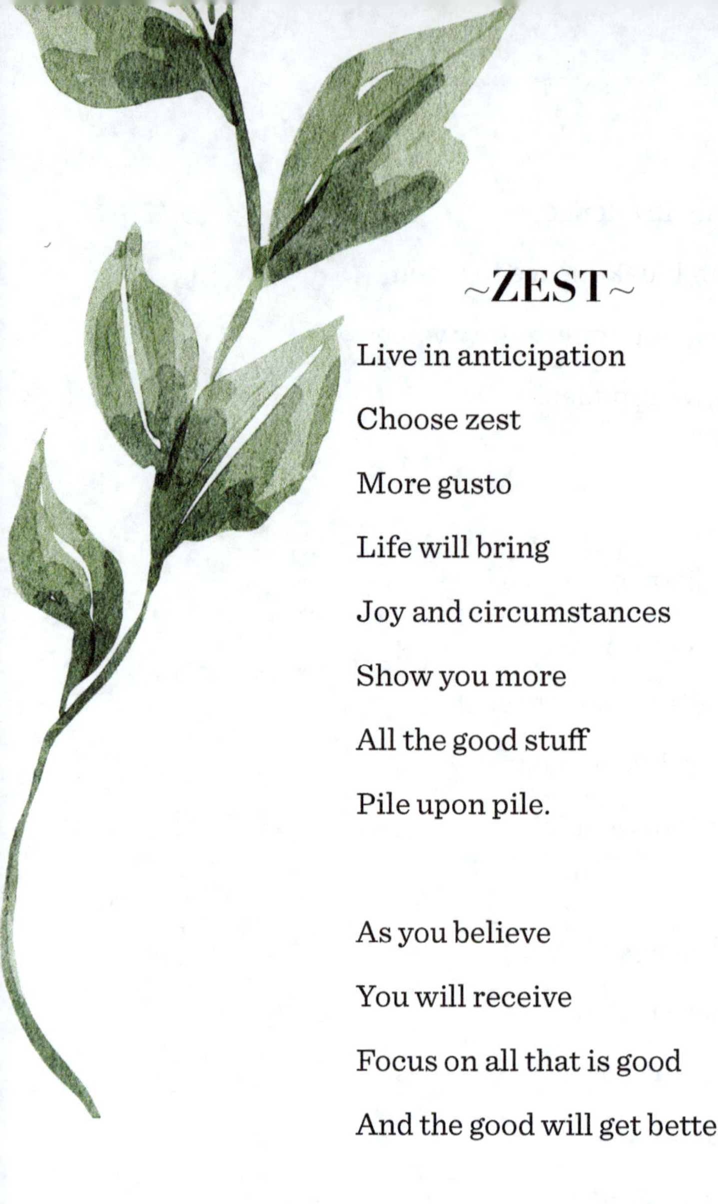

~ZEST~

Live in anticipation

Choose zest

More gusto

Life will bring

Joy and circumstances

Show you more

All the good stuff

Pile upon pile.

As you believe

You will receive

Focus on all that is good

And the good will get better.

Angels will prepare the way

As you desire.

All that is harmonious

All that is healthy.

Your emotional state of mind

What you think

What you believe

Becomes reality.

Emotions will trigger

More of the good

Or

More of where you have been

Get your emotions right.

Feel the best feelings

Lead with gratitude

Only good thoughts

Train your mind.

Reset and refocus

Trial and error

A learning process

A thinking process

A believing process

A receiving process

All up to you.

~JOYFUL AMBIVALENCE~

Living in uncertainty

No care either way

Chasm of indifference

Straddling the fence.

Low importance

Just indifferent

No psychosis here.

Just ambivalent to an outcome

In my defense.

On my list of priorities

This will not rank

No second thoughts

No reason to fret

Or find perplexing.

Ambivalent admonition

Scolding and warning

I care neither way.

Joyous and carefree

Two shits I do not give.

I left you for a reason

I left of my own volition

Joy turned its face in my direction

Made the transition

Now I live happily ever after

With my joyful decision.

~DID I LISTEN?~

Did I listen to my gut?

To my inner voice

And admonitions?

The headstrong

Capable

Part of me

Moving ahead

At breakneck speed.

Did I once stop?

Ask for divine intervention

To guide my way

Guide my direction?

Or did I plunge headlong

No compass

No concern

For consequences

Of my actions?

Did I know it all

Believing in my efforts

To overcome

To manage the inevitable fall?

If I knew then

What I know now

Would I listen more

Would I wait for answers?

Or would I be me

All over again

Hoping for a different answer

Hoping for a different then?

Pause and reflect

Then and now

Choices and consequences

Obedience to my will.

Intentional or unintentional

A parable in my name

Disputes of my soul

Would remain the same.

~NAYSAYERS~

Negative naysayers

Throwing a punch

Duck when it comes flying

Your direction.

Get out of the way

Barbs of fire

Going to catch you

On the chin.

Lies

All untrue

Nothing personal

Just a bit of vective

To harm your ego.

You got into

That ring,

And others will say

You did not earn it

Or earn your way.

Rubbish

Throw it away

Messages not meant for you,

Just reflections

Of their tiny souls.

All muck and mire

Distorted views

Those souls are empty

Nothing to you.

Consciously choose which parts of you to cultivate and which parts to let go. Let go of what doesn't serve you any longer, let go of friendships that you have outgrown and let go of expectations that no longer belong to you.

~**PINING**~

Pining for something else

Obscure and elusive

Destination focus

Missing the here and now.

Looking forward

Looking back

Mindless one track

Off track

Missing the real track.

The race to the end

Began with the race to win

As if the win

Was all that mattered

All that existed

To the very end.

Your compass

Corrupted

Missing what matters.

~PERECTIONIST ~

This need to be perfect

Started when young

To please a parent

Always do right

Never let them down.

Perfection a rule

Imperfection a constant

Finding the balance

Try to get it right

Instead, get it wrong.

Kicking yourself

Picking yourself

To death and bones

This desire to always get it right

On the first go round

Unreasonable

Delusional.

Sets a child up for doom

For failure

Feared the most.

Definition of perfection

Different to most.

Others cannot measure up

To such exacting

Never good enough

Remorse.

Please an adult

A child pretends

Untrue to self

Learns to please others

Attain the domain...

Of perfect friend

Of perfect daughter

Of perfect wife

Of perfect mother

A perfect life.

Ain't no such thing

Definition of perfection
Is not meant for anyone
Throw that dingleberry in the trash.

Parents were wrong

Demanding in so many ways

To expect perfection

Without delay.

Just a child

A child should play.

Not worry about pleasing a parent

Hoping a friend might stay.

A desperate attempt

Believing it true

Perfection is not God like

We are not meant to

Live with so many rules.

Commandments be damned

Just a child

A human.

Perfection is not a rule.

Meant to get it wrong

Again and again.

The only perfection

Is the illusion

Of pretend.

~CANVAS~

My life

A canvas

Each waking hour

Each soul I meet

Let them know

While my years are diminishing

My heart is expanding

Until the very last breath

I will fully embrace

Create anew

As if just beginning

My gift of life

Is

Right where I am.

~LEVEL UP~

You keep trying to remind me

Entice me to return

Insinuate yourself into my present

While trying to leave the past

In the past.

Each time I try to level up

Move forward with momentum

You move mountains

Closer

To obstruct.

The you

Is me

And the me

Gets in my own way.

Lessons uniquely mine

Will continue to return

Until my level

Is leveled up

And those mountains

No longer obstruct.

~WHISPERS OF
MY SOUL~

My friends support

And honor

My soul when it whispers

No matter the rough

Rendition it sings.

Sometimes it whispers

Sometimes it yells

To be free of all

The noise

The world sells.

Quiet whispers

Speak to my soul

A soft hand touches

And reminds me

To listen

Let go of control.

If not for the whispers

Of my soul

I would soon forget

Soon, lose control.

As I connect

Soul to soul

Friend to friend

We share each other's whispers

Each other's souls.

~THISTLE~

A memory

A thistle

Pricked my hand

So, I let it go,

To blow

To blunder

Swept up in the wind,

Where all memories flow.

Did the thistle choose me?

Or

Did I choose the thistle?

As with memories,

Did my memories choose me?

Or

Did I choose my memories?

Only the thistle knows...

Each petal

Dithering in the current.

My hand will heal,

To pick another thistle.

~HASTE YE BACK~

In my haste

Forgot to laugh

Relish this moment

Taste with vigor

Of bitter

Of sweet

Essence to linger.

See it like it is

Embellished with sprinkles

Life giving light

This moment

In memory

Never forgotten.

I took the time

To live in the present

To live in the now.

Ears meant to hear

Nothing but quiet.

As my soul delights

Praise to the ether

Haste ye back

And succumb to this moment.

BITS AND BOBS

~BIRDS~

Each bird a different tune

A tiny chorus

For me and for you.

A trill

A trong

A different song.

Together they sing

Tring a ling ling.

And the music they create

A morning filled with song

Magic with their prose,

Magic with their praise.

~MY GARDEN~

I love as my garden

Blooms and blooms

Roses all bundled

Nestled in their petals.

Seeds of various

Fruit and flower

Emerging from soil

Planted with hope.

My babies are sprouting

Sprinkle with water

Each day a new seedling

Sprouts a new flower.

My gardenia

White blossoms

Fills the air.

Sweet peas trailing

Wafting in the breeze

Smell them as they bloom

Down the street.

Mint trails wild

Varities in the mix

Fresh herbs for cooking

Rosemary for homemade bread.

Tomatoes

Eat from the vine

Strawberries so lucious

Raspberries divine.

Can't pick them fast enough

Eating in the garden

Earth to table

Not forgotten.

Solace in my garden

God's nature reserve

Keeps me grounded

Part of the earth.

Perfectionism is an illusion.
Unless it is tiramisu.
Perfect tiramisu is no illusion.

~CAT~

She nudges

For one more pet

This cat of mine

Likes her scratches.

All around her ears

And under her chin.

Purring all the while

Daily dose of oxytocin

Getting her fix.

A lovely creature

This cat of mine

Indignant on her own

Until she wants a bit of attention.

Some scratches

Along her back

On her belly

Nibbles my hand.

Darts off in exasperation

When she has to share

Morning lovin' with the other cat.

~TEXAS HOME~

Amarillo to Houston

What a drive

North to South

East to West

Texas, takes her time.

Spring in Texas

Glorious poppies

Sunflowers for bonnets

Yellows, blues and browns

Bluebonnets spreading

Purple the ground.

Butterflies and wildlife

Feed from Spring

Carry their young

South

Through Texas.

Creatures migrate,

Milkweed for Monarchs

And nectar for bees.

Flat desert to hill country

Lush farms of San Anton.

Cattle graze fields

Native grass only grown.

And corn shoots up fast

Waving, incessant breeze

Native Texas

Vast and uncertain

Reminds travelers to revel

In God's natural heaven.

~TIME OF YEAR~

Just once a year

Festive altercations and family near

Breaking bread together

No loneliness, only cheer.

Baking goodies for colleagues

Just one request

And the sweets are out

Enjoying together.

Cuz we break bread together

No matter the distance

Love travels

Sweets make the difference.

Missing them all

Good times we had

Laughter made the days

What we feel in our hearts

Never says goodbye.

~CONSTERNATION~

Consternation

What the heck?

I just don't get it

Disconnect.

You lost a wheel

Your tire is rolling

One is missing

You only have three.

You let him change

Your tires at home

Forgot the lugnuts

Tightened

All but one.

Cuz he got distracted

Didn't finish the job.

Now you are stranded

You lost that tire

Rolling down the road.

Jolted to your senses

You just drove ten miles

On lugnuts not tightened

Lopsided down the road.

You forgot to check his work

Trusted in his armor

Once a safe journey

Intentional or not.

So, now you worry

Sitting in the middle of the intersection

How he forgot

To keep you safe.

Lucky for you

Happenstance

You know how to drive

Three wheels to chance.

Your soul is on a healing journey.

Every lesson and encounter is an opportunity to become whole.

~DEVIL'S LETTUCE~

Been smokin' some reefer

Pairs well with wine

End of my workday

Feelin' the breeze

Pungent and wafting

As I toke and breathe.

Rolled at my desk

Took a few hits

On my way home

Anticipating

The sense of relief.

Powerful stuff

Legal of course

Bought some at the pharmacy

Hefty tax

Without a prescription

Can get expensive

If you aren't into medicine.

Munchies at night

Bong or pipe

Prefer them rolled in cigars

A fatty

Nice and tight.

Indica for sleep

Sativa at my desk

We gather to break bread

And pass one together.

Sharing a doobie

Passing it around

Weed, reefer, bud

We can all expound

On the merits of pot

Smiles abound.

My friends hide from their kids

Take it for sleep

Until daddy ate too many

Asking for relief.

Now dad's a stoner

Mom likes the sex.

Budnicians suggest

A hybrid or three

Edible and chocolate

Brownies too.

Edibles with caution

Take a while to kick in

You think you haven't eaten enough

Until you trippin'.

You took the whole damn gummy

Cuz you couldn't wait

Now your head is muddled

Crawling in disgrace.

Knees to the floor

Enjoy this rare moment

You took a hit too many

Edibles to explore

Brownies on the inside

Munchies galore.

~INTERSTELLAR PHENOMENON~

I totally believe

Even though I've never seen

Objects floating in the sky

Darting in between.

Seams in our universe

Magnificent to imagine

From depths of the ocean

This place we call home.

Center of the earth

Hovering in sacred

Fields and streams

Objects free to roam.

Yes, Yes

I do believe.

In the unseen

Uncanny

Surreal.

Silently watching

From afar

A different dimension

A fold in our sky

Alternate universe.

Our folly to assume

We are alone

And at the center

Of one great cataclysm

We call home.

God's dimension

We are meant to explore

Only we perceive

A fragment of time

But, there is more.

A tiny resolution

Vast worlds

Not of our understanding.

Open wide

Your mind to explore,

Beyond comprehension

Evolve into

Expansive wonders.

Open your mind

Willingness

To understand

There is more.

~PICKLE JUICE~

Salt and brine

Greets my taste buds.

I drink pickle juice

All the time.

Dill pickles

Munchies on the side

Nothing sweet about them

Just sour brine.

Dried up pickles

macerate in the jar.

Not because I'm pregnant

Just enjoy the taste.

Frustration for my family

Straight from the jar.

As kid I loved

A jar of my own.

Must have been a nutrient

Lacking at home.

Now I enjoy

A bit in my cocktail.

Makes a martini

A bit splashy

A bit sour

Matches the olive

And pickle juice

At the five o'clock hour.

~AN OLD FRIEND CALLING~

An old friend calling

To lighten my day

Remembering good times together

Las Vegas and gambling

Our folly

Never delayed.

Roller coasters and fine dining

Room service for five

Laughter and giggles

Our lives

Together, we inspired.

Catching up

Simple things

Remind us to remember

Friends for a lifetime

Make the journey

Twice the better.

~LIPSTICK~

Red, pink or blush

Gloss, matte or lush

My lips get the color

I deserve the most.

Work, play or date

Lips ornate

Luscious smackers

Kissable tenders.

Colors showcase

My bottom lip

Fully dressed

Ready for the world.

Natural all the time

No use for fillers

Plump enough

Rain, sun and shine.

My lips so soft

Illuminated in red

Latching to his lower lip

Matching endeavor.

In someone else's rendition of a story, I'm probably the asshole.

In someone else's rendition of a story, I'm probably the asshole.

In someone else's rendition of a story, I'm probably the asshole.

In someone else's rendition of a story, I'm probably the asshole.

In someone else's rendition of a story, I'm probably the asshole.

In someone else's rendition of a story, I'm probably the asshole.

~**JO**~

Wood sage and sea salt

Bergamot oud

She created my favorite

Essence

Perfume for my soul.

Orange blossoms for lotion

Myrrh and tonka in black

Velvet rose and Oud

Pomegranate noir.

Jo, Jo, Jo,

Perfume for my soul.

~THE SPOT~

Patient and waiting

He emptied his cart

Took forever

An eternity in slow motion.

My blinker clearly blinking

Peripheral vision

Watching it unfold

As little miss

Sports car

Stole my anticipated spot.

Ms. zippity zoom

Doo daa'd my chosen spot

As if invisible

Entitled,

So clever

She zippity doo daa'd

In haste.

Not to underestimate

Granny old lady

Merciful me

Found a nearby spot.

Out of spite

Conveniently trailed

Behind her

Pushing my cart.

Close on her heels

She suddenly stopped

Oops, my cart

Zippity doo daa'd into her backside,

Caught from behind,

Down she went.

Off I scampered

Zippity doo daaing my way

Back to my chosen spot.

~GOT LUCKY~

Count myself lucky

Among many my age,

Still be driving

Yet forget

Where I parked.

Keys in hand

Rows upon rows,

Trying to recall,

Which direction

I entered

And landed.

Dismayed by my resilience

To stand in one place

And replay my mind,

Digression

Regression

Where did I park?

~SHAME AND BLAME~

Shame and blame

All the attributes of

An adversarial game

To keep you mired

In ego

Mind Altering

Heart wrenching pain.

~QUARTERVOIS~

My misgivings

Drought in my soul

Chasm of indifference

Straddling the fence.

And my propensity to ask

When, when, when

Maybe then, maybe then.

Unnerving.

Possibly missing the message

Sorrows woeful yet benign

Turning each page

Umbilical cord to my soul.

Sets me in a new direction

Evolve or repeat

Evolve or repeat.

Incantations of my soul.

(n.) crossroads, turning point in one's life. The moment you change
your life. The moment you transition.

~THIRTEEN MINUTES~

Thirteen minutes

Your soul lifting

A new journey awaits

Thirteen minutes to resuscitate.

780 seconds

Reviewing your life

Your mistakes.

And when it all ended

Back to life you came

Your soul joined the living

Now awake.

Tell me dear,

All those seconds

No time to waste.

Thirteen minutes

God took your hands

Second chances

Make haste.

~RENDITION~

Each rendition

A different color

Midnight blue to aqua

Watercress to vibrant green.

I am those colors

Sparkling

Darkly

Different in the light.

Each minute of each day

Chasm of colors

Stretching to find the way

Sentimental colors

Bring me together

Merging my whitest

Filtering my darkest.

All of my colors

Shining

Unmuted

Renovating my rendition.

~WANKER~

Wee Willy wanker

Stepped out for a pint

The pub he knew

With all the brew

And mates to share a yarn.

Little did he know

So, he liked to blow

Words of sage advice.

Everyone knew

His tiny brain

Matched the tool in his trousers.

His wife at home

Glad he was gone

A few hours of respite from his banter.

Drunk he would come

Home for a slumber,

Nary a word to mutter

Upon his head

The stairs he would saunter,

Falling up,

Falling down

Cursing he would utter.

Until the next mourn,

Leaving the door

Wide open,

As he strode the same path

To bellow,

And share words of meaningless

Dribble with his mates.

~APRIL EIGHTH~

A total eclipse

Not of my heart

Happens but once in a lifetime

I learned

Not to trust.

I put on magic spectacles

To shield from the rays

The brightness too hard to gaze.

But my heart still lingers

Waiting for that eclipse

Turning my world

Into darkness for a bit.

The sun and moon pass by earth

About the same time.

Maybe in my next lifetime

My heart may be ready

To turn around

And look at the sky

Knowing I gave it my best

Sun and moon to inspire.

~DIDDLY SQUAT
AND JACK DIDDLY~

Diddly Squat and Jack Diddly

Went for a country drive

No destination in mind

Squat forgot the map

And Jack was happy to dally.

Together the pair lost their way

No interest in destination

Happily forgetful,

Blissfully unaware.

No plan in the making

No thought for their welfare.

Just two chump buddies

Happy to do squat

Jack and his Diddly

Diddly and his Squat.

A pair to remember

Not giving a thought

Their life as a whole

Did not mean a lot.

Others were quick to recall

A life measured by small

Dillying around

Not doing squat.

Their drive in the country

No map brought along

Content to rely

To lose focus and fall.

Together they bumbled

Stumbled and drove

Got on a few ferries

Ended up in the Hebrides

Isle of Skye.

While one dillied

The other did Jack

They both dallied

And never looked back.

~TODAY~

Today

I today'd

Enough today'ing

For the day.

Until tomorrow's today

When I will do

Today once more.

About the Author

Skeeter Smith is an author and poet. Her first book of poetry, Musings and Meanderings Book 1, explored a lifetime of painful yet humorous experiences. In Poetic Fragments of My Imagination Book 2, her free verse poems invite readers to share her vulnerability and offer a path toward healing. Her poetry is much like her life - open and transparent. Skeeter's most important accomplishments are within the four walls of her home. She is a dedicated single mother and grandmother of three. She holds a Bachelor of Arts in History from Arizona State University, and a Master of Business Administration.

Skeeter's poetry appeared in a Texas literary magazine. She is an award-winning short story author in San Antonio and an active member of writing guilds throughout the state. Skeeter is currently writing a series of five historical novels. Her first in the series, Nordic Girl, will be released in late 2026.